student loans pros and cons

by SIMON JENKINS and BILL VAN STRAUBENZEE

Conservative Political Centre

In common with other CPC publications, this pamphlet is a personal contribution to discussion and not an official Party pronouncement.

CPC Number 415

Published by the Conservative Political Centre, 32 Smith Square, London SW1 and printed by Oliver Burridge and Co. Ltd., Crawley, Sussex.

First published September 1968
SBN 85070 415 4

RT. HON. SIR EDWARD BOYLE, Bart, MP

foreword

THE expansion of higher education, sometimes criticised as over-rapid, has in fact been one of Britain's major national achievements during the 1960s. It was rendered essential by the dramatic growth of the sixth forms during the 1950s, yet it could not have happened but for the greatly increased sums of money authorised by the Conservatives during the 'Macmillan era'.

Improved standards of school education, as well as larger age-groups, will always throw up increasing numbers of qualified entrants for higher education. And its continued expansion cannot be held back unless a Government were to be prepared, as a matter of deliberate policy, either to take steps to slow down the growth of the sixth forms, or to allow competition for university entry to grow still more severe – an alternative decisively, and rightly, rejected by the Robbins Committee.

However there is, of course, one major obstacle – the mounting cost. Hence this careful examination, which I greatly welcome, by Simon Jenkins and Bill van Straubenzee of a proposal that is frequently advanced in order to ease the budgetary impact of expanding higher education, namely the introduction of a system of student loans to cover the cost of maintenance.

It is important to recognise the extent to which both writers are in agreement over objectives. They are both concerned with the function of the education service as a means of levelling up opportunity. But Simon Jenkins, who has already made a notable contribution to Conservative Party thinking on the organisation of secondary education, is concerned lest the 'very high maintenance element in the cost of an additional place in higher education (should act) as a powerful disincentive to further expansion'. And he argues that a loans scheme, of the kind he advocates, could result in increased resources becoming available to other, more needy, parts of the education service: 'The object of this whole exercise is redistributive towards those deficiencies of the education service that most affect the working classes'.

In his reply, Bill van Straubenzee contests the proposition that we should find the money to remedy those deficiencies 'by severing the ladder of opportunity at the age of eighteen . . . It is no good', he says, 'encouraging children from low income families to stay on at school if you are going to slam the door in their face at the precise moment when they are in need of tangible financial assistance'. He also feels that sophisticated economic arguments in favour of student loans can cause us to lose sight of the essential point: 'In discussing loans the danger is that we are drawn into obstruse arguments about cost-benefit analysis, lifetime earnings, etc., when what really matters is equality of opportunity'.

It is because of the need to widen opportunity, and to foster ability wherever it is found, that the conclusion of the Robbins Committee still seems to me cogent: 'On balance we do not recommend immediate recourse to a system of financing students by loans. At a time when many parents are only just beginning to acquire the habit of contemplating higher education for such of their children, especially girls, as are capable of benefiting by it, we think it probable that it would have undesirable incentive effects'. But it will do no service to anyone if Governments reject student loans, only to provide inadequate grants; that is why the Conservative Opposition, in view of the Government's indiscriminate 50 per cent cuts in the scale of increases recommended by the Brown Committee, have advocated a special review of student grants to be carried out next year.

I hope this pamphlet will be widely read.

Edward Boyle

introduction

UNIVERSITIES in the United Kingdom are financed from two sources: central government grants paid direct to individual universities through the University Grants Committee, and fees paid by local authorities for particular students within their areas. UGC grants contribute about 90 per cent of the cost of university education while fees provide the remaining 10 per cent. Other institutions of higher education – colleges of education, polytechnics and colleges of technology – are financed through local authorities, though some colleges of education receive grants direct from the central government.

The students within these institutions therefore pay no money themselves for their courses of study, except for the small proportion of students (about 5 per cent) whose parents' income is above the maximum for payment of fees, and those overseas students not supported through some official channel.

In addition, all students engaged upon a recognised full-time course of study, receive a maintenance award to cover living costs during that course of study. The maintenance grant payable by the LEA[1] is related to the income of the student's parents with the result that no maintenance grant is received when adjusted family income is over £4,200. Out of the maintenance grant must come not just food, clothing and books, but also travel to and from home and to and from university buildings and, increasingly important, hall charges or rent for a flat. The maintenance grant system was introduced on a national basis after the war with the intention of easing the passage into higher education of boys and girls from working class backgrounds. Prior to the last war they received assistance, but in the form of scholarships which were often inadequate to support them – particularly when their parents had to keep them in the vacation. The present system of higher education awards in Britain is unique in the Western world – no other country provides the

[1]Local Education Authority.

same degree of student support. Even in Eastern Europe, where a complex system of scholarships operates, it is doubtful if students enjoy quite the financial freedom they do here. One result of this is certainly the fact that a higher proportion of students in higher education in Britain come from working class backgrounds than in any other Western country. And, although the figures are most deceptive, it is probable that we do every bit as well in this respect as the Communist nations, where part-time and correspondence students are included in higher education totals. However, the figure for universities alone is less encouraging. The research of the Robbins Report on higher education[1] showed that the proportion of university students from working class homes was about the same in the early 'sixties as in the early 'forties. It is true that before the war most working class students could obtain scholarships and the actual number of undergraduates from such families has risen considerably. But on Robbins' estimates, the universities remain strongly middle class institutions. To increase the proportion of undergraduates from the lower end of the social scale therefore remains an important objective.

The cost of higher education

Calculation of the cost of higher education and its various components is complicated by the wide definition it is given. It is nowadays taken to include not just universities (financed through the UGC) and colleges of education (financed partly through the Department of Education and partly through local authorities) but also the proposed polytechnics (financed through LEAs) and any 'advanced work' in colleges of technology. Student awards for 1968-9 from local authorities and DES[2] total £130m. (of which university awards take roughly half). This figure includes the cost of fees, which are paid direct to the universities and are never seen by the student; the proportion of awards taken for fees is about £30m. but fees are small in terms of the cost of a degree course (about 10 per cent of it).

Higher education as a whole costs this year approximately £710m. of which about £100m. or 14 per cent goes on student maintenance. Universities alone cost £236m. Current expenditure on higher education has been increasing annually at a rate of something like 12 per

[1] *Report of the Committee on Higher Education* (1963).

[2] Departments of Education and Science.

cent since 1960 – capital expenditure by much more. The expectation is that this rate of increase will slacken to about 6 per cent per annum as more school leavers are admitted, if not to universities, then to colleges of education and technology. Higher education grew relatively slowly compared with the primary and particularly the secondary school system after the war. It was not until the pressure on places grew in the early 1960s and the Robbins Report forecast a massive increase in demand that the Government planned to expand the universities. The fact that higher education has thus been expanding at roughly twice the rate of growth of the rest of the education system since 1960 is understandable. Whether it can justify a high growth rate into the 1970s – as it must if it is both to meet the demand and maintain present standards – is in part what this pamphlet is about. The rapid increase in the numbers in the sixth forms is going to raise demand for higher education far faster than the growth in size of each age group. The education they will be demanding is, in terms of quality of facilities, staff/pupil ratio and scale of maintenance support, probably the best in the world. It is also one of the most 'efficient', in terms of low failure and wastage rates and shortness and intensity of courses – though this is in part due to sixth form specialisation and due to the severe competition for places, at least in universities.

Meeting the cost

The current economic difficulties facing the government have drawn attention to all sectors of government expenditure including higher education. An indication of this has been the unwillingness of the government to ensure that student grants keep up with the rise in the cost of living. Whatever the basis for the 1965 assessment, there is no doubt that the present grant level is way behind the rise in living costs since then. The latest blow at the maintenance grant came with the Government's action in cutting by half the increase in maintenance awards proposed by the advisory panel under Professor A. J. Brown. From October 1968 the £370 maintenance award at Oxford, Cambridge and London will go up to £395 and the £340 award at other universities will rise to £360.

Meanwhile the pressures among a number of economists and particularly within the Department of Education itself for a complete overhaul of the maintenance grant system have become considerable. The initial floating of the idea of a 'loan element' in grants by Mr Anthony Crosland in 1966 met with a frosty reception from the students, largely because at the time there seemed no sense in the reform. Since the announcement that current expenditure on education over the next two years will rise 2½ per cent less than originally planned, more people have been taking a critical look at higher education in general and student grants in particular. With a projected rate of increase in expenditure on education as a whole of 3½ per cent in 1969-70, and the certainty that the Treasury will endeavour to keep it near that target in successive years, an item that is likely to increase at some 6 per cent per annum inevitably comes under scrutiny.

There are many ways in which money can be saved in the higher education sector. Government spokesmen have talked ominously about the 'luxurious' staff/student ratio, about the 'expense' of having students living away from home, about the need to economise in the use of 'university plant', and about such schemes as the Box and Cox idea in colleges of education. But the proposal that has been most widely debated – and the one which would probably yield the largest apparent saving – has been that the student maintenance award should be replaced or reduced by the introduction of some arrangement whereby its cost is recouped by repayment by graduates. We examine here various schemes, either in practice elsewhere or proposed or merely conjectured, for student loans.

Loan proposals

The most important criterion by which different schemes are distinguished is the simple one of how much money does the Government wish to recoup from the higher education budget. Some wish to see a loan scheme covering the total cost of higher education (which, including the colleges of technology 'advanced work', would amount to £710m. a year). Such an extreme proposal would certainly impose a penal burden on the young graduate and make many, even those likely to be well paid, think seriously about whether higher education is worth it. Others confine the repayment to the university sector (running at nearly £250m. next year), or to current expenditure alone – arguing that the state should provide the 'social capital' of the education system, but individuals the current cost of their education. This would leave most students with a debt to repay of up to £3,000 on graduation – more for science students.

But few would really hold that the vast bulk of university income, the UGC subvention, should be repaid by graduating students. This would impose on the young graduate population a very substantial burden. It would also offend against the principle that state provided education should be free of charge, a principle that is applied in every other sector of the education service.

A second alternative would be for loans to replace the maintenance grant and the fees paid by the LEAs. This would save the Government about £130m. per year or 6.5 per cent of the national education bill. Fees are extremely difficult to estimate since they vary widely depending on the institution and the subject studied. They amount to about £75 per year at many universities. So in addition to his debt of nearly £1,200 for maintenance the student would have to borrow £225 for fees making a total of £1,425 for a three-year course.

The chief target for most advocates of student loans is the maintenance grant, ranging from £50 up to £395 a year depending on the type of institution attended, and the income level of the student's parents. The means test is now less rigorous than it was before 1962. A proportion of the grant only starts to be paid by the parent when adjusted income (income after allowing for certain items like dependants, pension contributions and mortgage interest) rises above £900. As a result, even among the predominantly middle class university sector, only 5 per cent of students find themselves in receipt of no maintenance grant at all. The total cost of student maintenance (not fees) is in 1968-9 approximately £100m., equivalent to 5 per cent of national expenditure on education. The figure is likely to rise to £112m. following implementation of the grant increases in October 1968.

There has also been talk, particularly in Government circles, of the possibility of a 'loan element' being introduced into the grant system. Loans have been suggested for post-graduate students, an increasing sector of the student population. It has been suggested that any further increases in the student grant to keep student income in line with the cost of living should take the form of a loan rather than a grant. And loans have also been advocated for alleviating cases of hardship – a practice already adopted on a very small scale by some local authorities. Depending on one's point of view such proposals look very much like the thin end of the wedge, or a half-hearted attempt in which the effort involved is not worth the return. The less significant loans are in student finance, the weaker will be the arguments against them. But the less important they are, the weaker will be arguments in favour since the financial savings consequent upon their introduction would be minimal.

Type of scheme

To an extent the type of scheme advocated depends on the level of return required. A major saving will need a severe scheme. Broadly speaking there are two basic types of scheme: first the straight loan on a quasi-commercial basis; second a loan repayable by instalments related to income in later life. The first of these two schemes is the type employed almost universally overseas. The student borrows a sum of money to see him through university or college which must be paid back within a fixed period at a certain rate of interest. One example of this type is the National Defence Student Loan programme which operates in the USA.

National Defence Student Loans

An eligible undergraduate may borrow up to $1,000 each academic year to a maximum of $5,000. The student must begin repayment nine months after he leaves college. Interest on the loan is 3 per cent per year on the amount outstanding but only commences when repayment begins. Repayment may be extended over a maximum period of ten years. Instalments are deferred and interest is not payable up to a total of three years while the borrower is serving in the US Armed Forces or in the Peace Corps. Instalments are also deferred and interest is not payable as long as the student is in full or half-time attendance at an institution of higher education.

If a borrower becomes a full-time teacher in a public or non-profit school, college or university, up to 50 per cent of the loan is forgiven at the rate of 10 per cent for each year of his teaching service. 100 per cent of the loan may be cancelled at the rate of 15 per cent a year for teaching service in 'hardship schools'.

It is the colleges themselves which approve, make and administer the loans. The institutions select suitable students to receive loans and are responsible for all matters of administration and repayment. The programme is almost completely commercial in character, except for the interest subsidy. The borrower signs a promissory note for his loan and repayment terms are contractual. The American student is under a commercial obligation to begin instalments nine months after he leaves college. It is his worry to make sure he is earning enough at that time to pay the instalments required.

Institutions are finding that repayment defaulters are a problem and special procedures have been designed to cope with them. The loan application form demands sufficient personal information about the student to enable the authorities to trace him in the event of default. The institution may take legal action when an instalment is more than sixty days overdue; legal proceedings and judgement are the same as in the case of a private commercial debt.

The most authoritative condemnation of the above type of student loan was made by Professor A. R. Prest in *Financing University Education*[1]:

> 'Nevertheless, the objections to this system as a main source of finance seem overwhelming. First, any such system is likely to be far more of a deterrent to a boy from a poor family contemplating university education than to a rich one, even if the element of subsidy is graduated inversely with parental incomes. Readiness to shoulder the burden of repayment is likely to be much less in the case of a student without the possibility of financial backing from his parents. Secondly, the term of repayment will be the same irrespective of whether a man receives an injury in his early manhood which incapacitates him for life or whether he feels a call to enter a low-income profession or whether he becomes a modern Henry Ford or John D. Rockefeller. So the risk of putting a millstone round one's neck is really considerable and must rule out heavy reliance on any such policy for achieving the objectives we have put forward.'

It must be said at the same time that without them, thousands of American working-class students would never have gone to college at all. The same goes for loan schemes in Scandinavia and elsewhere, where loans are looked upon as liberation for poor children. However, in 1966 the American Federal Government introduced student grants for the first time in order to support some poor school leavers for whom loans were not a solution.

Variable repayable advances

A more equitable loan scheme has been proposed by a number of economists and educationists in the United Kingdom, taking account of the progress already made in making higher education free and open to all. The most favoured scheme is that presented to the Robbins Committee and printed in its Appendix. It was pre-

[1]Institute of Economic Affairs, 1966.

pared by Professor A. R. Prest and was later expanded in *Financing University Education*. Prest suggests a system of 'variable repayable advances' – or what amounts to an earmarked tax on graduates. The student would borrow money in the same way but repayment would be related to income in later life. Professor Prest suggests that repayment would begin only after the graduate's income had exceeded a certain level. The threshold at which instalments begin would be adjusted according to the graduate's family responsibilities. However, once the income threshold is passed the graduate pays a percentage of his income towards the cost of his higher education. Professor Prest intends this graduate tax to be collected by PAYE throughout the graduate's career until he reaches sixty-five. In this way graduates whose salaries remain near the threshold may never repay at all, while those whose incomes rise to £10,000 or £20,000 a year may repay their higher education costs several times over. Presumably, actuarial calculations could be made to ensure that each generation as a whole pays off the total cost of its higher education.

There are several important disadvantages to the system outlined above. Variable repayable advances must continue to be repaid over a period of more than forty years after graduation. Forty years from now this form of taxation is going to look as antiquated as the Window Tax. Moreover, since the tax is to be spread over such a long period, the annual repayments would be small and it would be many years before the Government recouped the amount spent on educating each student. Professor Prest's system would therefore not provide the immediate budgetary relief which is the prime argument in favour of student loans.

Repayments would not be limited to the amount originally borrowed. Hence a student who thought himself likely to earn a high salary after graduation would avoid Professor Prest's unlimited repayments by borrowing a fixed sum commercially. This would reintroduce by the backdoor the serious disadvantages of the contractual loan system. The student would feel impelled to take the risk of repaying a fixed contractual debt rather than incur an open-ended tax burden which would last until he was sixty-five.

The graduate tax would be progressive and would therefore increase marginal rates of income tax above their present level. This runs counter to the widely accepted need to reduce the disincentive effect of high marginal rates of direct taxation.

Lastly, Professor Prest's system is politically the least acceptable. It does not seem fair that one section of the population should be obliged to undertake an unlimited commitment over a period of forty years, the total sum repaid perhaps having no relation to the original cost or actual benefit of the payer's higher education.

Throughout the rest of this pamphlet therefore we shall be discussing a modified version of Professor Prest's proposal, namely that repayments should be made via PAYE as soon as adjusted income reaches above a threshold but the total repaid by an individual student shall not exceed the amount that he originally borrowed, possibly allowing for interest.

Conclusion

Any major reform, particularly those involving a substantial change of principle in which a section of the community must sacrifice a measure of prosperity, is the cause of considerable acrimony and often misrepresentation on both sides. On the one hand it is easy to 'play priorities' against the otherwise entrenched position of one's opponent; on the other it is easy to shoot down a new idea with 'difficulties'. In this pamphlet we try to set out the arguments between advocates and opponents of student loans. Neither side would deny that the grants system in this country is in itself a good thing – an aspect of education in which the United Kingdom undoubtedly leads the world. Nor would they deny that the education service is going through a period of severe strain when some of its sectors will be seriously under-provided – not only primary and secondary education, but the universities and colleges themselves. We have tried therefore to eliminate overlap from the two cases presented here, and we have tried also to eliminate patent inconsistency. We leave you to choose between them.

SIMON JENKINS

the case *in favour* of student loans

I SHOULD make it plain from the start that I regard the provision by the state of higher education in precisely the same way as I regard primary and secondary education. It should be free of charge to everyone in all its basic respects – the buildings, equipment and the pay of teachers. This is true today except for the 5 per cent of students whose parents must pay fees to cover a small part of the cost and the 10 per cent of students who are from overseas who pay considerably more fees but many of whom are supported through some official channel. (To the extent that overseas students and their parents pay no taxes to the Exchequer their education in this country takes the form of aid and should be treated as such budgetarily.) The present system whereby local authorities pay for about 10 per cent of university provision through fees is an absurd and largely pointless complication of the issue of university financing, and it makes much harder the analysis of the cost of student maintenance since fees and maintenance are all included in statistics for 'awards to students'. My concern here is solely with the element of student support that pays for no part of university or college education but provides the student with an income while he is studying. This figure is approximately £100m. in the year 1968-9 for the maintenance of students in universities and colleges of education and technology, including post-graduates.

Why a loan?

The higher education sector of the education system has, since the early 1960s, carried a prestige unequalled by any other. From the establishment of the new universities, through the acceptance and surpassing of the Robbins targets (the only education report to which financial response has surpassed recommendation) right down to the extraordinarily lenient treatment of higher education in the February 1968 cuts, only the best has appeared to be good enough. In so far as this amounted merely to the making up of lost ground in the forties and fifties it was fair enough. Universities and colleges had received relatively little attention until Robbins came along. Now they are doing very nicely, and the spotlight has passed 'down the line' to the secondary schools (Newsom) and the primaries (Plowden), and soon, probably, to special education.

There are few who could deny that the deficiencies the spotlight has picked out are glaring ones. Above all else, attention has been drawn to the effect on educational attainment of social and environmental background. The Newsom Report[1] in the case of the secondary modern school early leaver and the Plowden Report[2] in the case of the slum primary school child presented a challenge to the educationist which he can only hope to meet, particularly in the case of Plowden, with the aid of massive financial resources. These resources have been conspicuously absent. Indeed, by cruel chance, just as our awareness of need is becoming more acute, economic circumstances have forced on us the demand that expansion of spending on education must over the next two years be cut back to the smallest increase for over a decade. These points are made because it is no good our saying, as many students have been saying, that the deficiencies in the education service are no business of theirs; the government must find the money itself. The government will *not* find the money, and primary and secondary education will have to go without.

There is at present a chronic imbalance in an educational system which favours those who stay the course to reach university or college, in effect at the expense of those who, for lack of adequate resources, drop out. The Crowther Report[3] showed that in the vast majority of cases early leaving could be attributed to parental pressure to produce a wage packet. A tiny proportion of working class families receive a totally unrealistic maintenance grant for a child staying on in the sixth form (very seldom is this more than £80 per annum). The great majority of students in higher education living at home receive £275 a year. Such a scale of priorities is absurd.

But the argument for asking higher education to make some contribution to bringing the privileged and the under-privileged sectors of the education service more into balance does not derive simply from the obvious need to spend more on our primary and

[1]*Half our future* (1963 .
[2]*Children and their primary schools* (1966).
[3]*Fifteen to eighteen* (1959).

secondary schools. Our present way of running and financing higher education was designed in a day when higher education was for a very small elite. We are now, according to Robbins, facing a situation in which by 1980 we shall have in full-time higher education 17 per cent of each age group; and this figure is now regarded as excessively conservative. It is certain that because of shortage of resources, both of capital and teachers, these students will be educated at a lower standard than at present. Official circles now regard it as inevitable that the marginal spending on extra students will decline sharply as staff/student ratios worsen and libraries and lecture halls cram fuller. But marginal expenditure on student maintenance cannot be reduced, without a severe lowering in living standards (as is admittedly happening at present). Unless the means test is extended or students are reduced to considerable poverty, spending on student support must rise much faster than current spending on higher education as a whole.

There can be no doubt that the very high maintenance element in the cost of an additional place in higher education acts as a powerful disincentive to further expansion. Many applicants whose qualifications would five years ago have assured them a place will have to be turned away. The present system of student support not only deprives primary and secondary education from more favourable treatment in the education budget, but by its inflexibility it restricts the expansion of higher education itself.

The total of £100m. spent on student support has in itself been increasing by an average of about 25 per cent a year since 1960, faster than any other major item of the education budget. Although the rate of increase will doubtless slow down as higher education numbers increase less rapidly, the maintenance grant has an uncomfortable tendency to rise faster even than student numbers. Between 1959 and 1966 numbers increased by 138 per cent, while the cost of keeping them went up by an astronomical 225 per cent (during which time the fee element in support declined proportionately!). It is clear that it is on the maintenance award rather than anything else that attention must be focused if money is to be saved and/or higher education expansion not seriously impeded.

The loan scheme

One way to save £100m. is simply not to spend it: to force students to return to sixth form status and live off their parents, attending the nearest university or college to their home. Or, if they prefer to go away to university, they may work in vacations or part-time during term to earn their keep or they may receive further parental support. This is the way students are educated in the vast majority of universities in the West. But it is clearly not the best way of studying, and is one that is quite unthinkable in Britain today. The alternative is to give the student the money required to maintain himself independent of his or her parents and ask that it be repaid later when the student has the means to do so. And it should be so constructed, first that a real saving takes place, and second, that repayment terms should not impose an unrealistic burden on the young graduate. The scheme proposed here is a variant on Professor Prest's scheme outlined in the introduction.

Students should receive their maintenance grants in the form of a loan up to a given maximum. The loan, which could be considerably more than the present grant (up to £450), should be repaid over a period that should vary dependent upon the graduate's income.

The details of the operation of a scheme such as this are clearly dependent above all on the extent to which the government of the day wishes to subsidise student support. There is little question of a loans scheme being workable; a variety of types work very well in Scandinavia and Germany, indeed in virtually all countries with a developed system of higher education. And students often leave higher education carrying and meeting, financial obligations which would make many British students blanch. If the Department of Education were to treat the £100m. they now spend on student support as a commercial outlay of capital yielding a rate of return when the loan fund reached a steady state as is the case in most overseas schemes, students could now be leaving university with the prospect of either some very heavy repayments in early years of employment or heavy interest charges on later repayments. There would also have to be recognition that defaulting would take place and hardship remission procedures would have to be established.

It would seem more just to reckon on the present subsidy for student support continuing until the loan fund reached a steady state with receipts in any one year equalling payments. For the fund to be self-financing with an increasing student population, it would be necessary to charge a rate of interest approximately equal to this rate of increase – though this might again be reckoned as subsidy (it would not be high).

A more complex issue is the subsidy required to cover special cases. Clearly again the 'severity' of the scheme directly dictates the possible savings. Different people may have different theories, and it is quite possible to evolve a loan scheme that reduces the sense of deprivation a graduate may feel to a minimum and still saves quite substantial sums of public money for other uses. My own bias is towards making a loans scheme as near self-financing as possible in the long term, partly because I want to redistribute educational resources towards the deprived sections of the service as much as possible, partly because it is fairer if some borrowers do not evade payment, and partly because some contingent benefits can arise from a fairly stiff scheme.

Repayment should take the form of a special graduate coding by the Inland Revenue on income tax – covering both PAYE and self-employed schedules. It might be fixed at 5 per cent of salary at £1,000 or above. The deduction would, of course, lapse when the principal had been paid off, which in the average case would at present take roughly twelve years. Graduates earning less than the minimum (which might in more lenient circumstances be fixed higher) would not start paying back until they reached it, and cases of special hardship – in which, for instance, family commitments unavoidably consumed all disposable income – would have to be allowed for. In the absence of interest charges a student postponing repayment would still pay the same total amount. The cost of delay would fall on the government.

Women will doubtless form the bulk of this category, and pose a major question for the operation of loan schemes in general. In Scandinavia and Germany there is a tradition that women enter employment during or after a university course and repayment of the loan is regarded as an accepted responsibility either by herself or by her husband – though a very substantial proportion of female students receive considerable family support at university. From an economic point of view the return on the higher education of women in Great Britain is very low indeed – partly through a general Western tradition that women do not work when they start a family and partly through the unresponsiveness of the economy to employing married women under different circumstances from men. There can be no doubt that the introduction of a loan scheme would be a powerful incentive both to getting highly qualified women into the labour force and to getting management and institutions better adapted to coping with wives with families as employees. From a repayment point of view, a wife who has not repaid any of her loan by the time she begins a family would have her repayment compounded with her husband's, and repayment would simply begin when his had finished. At any stage, payments could be made cancelling later repayments.

Clearly a number of implications would flow from these proposals, some important, some unpleasant to many students and some that can be seen as 'silver linings' to a necessary cloud.

Parental assistance

In the first place, there can be no doubt that the amount of family income attracted into supporting students at university would increase substantially, particularly in the case of girls. Over 60 per cent of students in higher education are from middle class homes, and while this does not necessarily mean wealthy homes, it does suggest a degree of commitment which might in a number of cases produce financial support rather than letting the student take out a full loan. Although this might reduce the sense of independence that exists at present for the student (which can carry its own disadvantages), there would be absolutely nothing to prevent any student taking a loan and the net effect would be pure gain to the education budget.

Student residence

There would also probably be a marked increase in students living at home, thus saving the most expensive item of the maintenance budget – rent or hall charges. The cost of residence has been exercising many university minds recently and a number of universities have looked more favourably on local applicants for this reason. There is considerable scope for exchanges between families with student children in mutually convenient towns. Living at home is not educationally ideal, but residence is becoming such a problem at present that any measure that alleviates it should be regarded with some favour.

Working class disincentive?

The major argument brought against loans is that they would penalise working class students. This would not be the case: loans would be free to all irrespective of family background. Although some upper-middle class parents might finance students themselves (as they do now) this would not affect the family of the working class loan-recipient. Indeed, the present grant system acts as far more of a penalty since it is inadequate and requires almost total support from families during vacations. On the related issue of incentive, however, it could be said that the working class family background is less conducive to entering upon education involving a major debt than it is when state support is forthcoming. However, in the first place, the repayment is an income related one – a very important point. In other words, it puts every student recipient of a loan on an equal footing on graduation. Secondly, as the Robbins Committee (which was receptive to the loans idea – but not just yet) suggested, working class families are getting more used to the idea of higher education as time goes on. And as others have pointed out, the idea of entering upon debt is hardly an alien one in these days of massive hire purchase.

But more important is the other Robbins argument – that the object of this whole exercise is redistributive *towards* those deficiencies of the education service that most affect the working classes. As Blaug has shown, we have an absurd system in this country which penalises the poor and deprived child all along the way, erecting immense educational and environmental hurdles in his path, only lavishing assistance on those who through supreme effort actually get through to the top. *A loan scheme of this kind cannot be opposed on egalitarian grounds.*

Student responsibility

One effect of the introduction of a loan scheme is one that perhaps finds little favour with students at present, but much more with their detractors. It is what Robbins called 'increasing individual responsibility'. As the report puts it: 'It is said that the student financed by grants is sometimes apt to take his privilege for granted; and that this may have as a by-product the lack of any particular sense of obligation and need to work'. The student financed by a loan 'knows that he has to pay the price later on and is therefore all the keener to get the most out of what he is buying'. Loans would certainly inject more of a vocational bias into much of higher education and make students more conscious of their responsibilities to contribute a return to society for the (still *free*) higher education they have received at its expense.

Attitudes to work

A corollary of this is the increase that would take place in industrial scholarships and other tied awards, which in turn would achieve a greater integration between universities and colleges and the world of industry and commerce – generally regarded as being a good thing. There would also be an expansion – though not necessarily – in the amount of vacation employment, and even term-time employment, undertaken by undergraduates.

Though students say this is a bad thing, and universities officially discourage it, the arrangements now made by the National Union of Students and by local students' unions for finding work for students, who appear to want something interesting to do as much as need the money, suggest that this is a development that is coming anyway. And there are as many who would argue that it is a very good thing for the student to learn 'what life is all about' by earning a wage packet while he is still studying. Again, the greatly increased demand for this type of employment would soon open up opportunities that now seem very few – as has been the case in the United States and Scandinavia where the tourist industry in particular is heavily dependent on student labour.

Brain drain

It is often argued that a loans scheme would be unfair in that those leaving the country would evade repayment. There is no reason why this should be the case. Indeed, one argument *for* loans is that those who benefit from our highly specialised higher education *should* put their services at the disposal of the nation or repay. And anyone leaving the country before repayment is complete must recognise a straightforward debt that must be repaid, either on departure or through arrangement with his new overseas employer. Such an arrangement is normal in the case of civil debts and inland revenue obligations – deliberate breaking of a legal obligation would not be common and the sanction of the courts if the defaulter returned would be available.

Student wastage

One question that has been raised by the loans issue is that of wastage. The UGC figures on this have now been published and are impressive or depressing depending on one's point of view. But one point is clear: comparison with wastage rates abroad is totally useless, since British experience is unique in that we have a greatly inflated demand over supply for university places – averaging out at roughly two applicants for every place. Competition is therefore severe and successful entrants are usually highly motivated – though this is by the same measure less true of colleges of education and technology.

There is sufficient evidence (Robbins) of an as yet still untapped reserve of ability in the schools such that there can be little question of demand for university places slackening off under a loans scheme. American and Scandinavian experience clearly illustrate this. It would remain a very good 'investment' to the individual. (If the individual did not think so then perhaps he or she is best not at university in the first place). The main point, however, is that there is no reason at all for wastage during courses to increase under a loans scheme since, if anything, the student should have more rather than less disposable income. If students choose to study on the cheap then that is their decision, but it is certainly not necessary for a student to be in financial straits. The loan is available to all.

Favoured employment

It has been suggested that loan repayments might be used to direct graduate labour into particular socially useful jobs. In Scandinavia it is common practice to waive repayments when graduates take teaching and related jobs in deprived areas of the country. My own bias is against distorting the basis of repayment within the administration of the scheme itself. Without raising the issue of the government distorting the professional labour market, it would be a mistake to waive repayments on a large scale since this would severely hinder the financial basis of the scheme. The simplest solution would be for straight bonuses to be offered for particular jobs, perhaps designed to cover loan repayments, but taking the form of salary increments – e.g. for teachers in slum schools. If industrial and commercial salaries became inflated to include 'fringe benefit' repayment arrangements, the net effect would be wholly beneficial: the graduate would be that much better off, the fund would get its money back quicker and private corporations would be making some direct contribution to the higher education system from which they had benefited immensely in terms of money saved from training.

Redistributing the savings

It has been suggested that difficulty might arise over the collection of repayments by the Inland Revenue as opposed to the Department of Education. Certainly the Revenue's record on earmarked revenue is not good (e.g. Road Traffic Fund). One solution is the Scandinavian and German one – to have students running the scheme themselves with a state grant to cover administrative costs. But this makes the graduated repayment scheme difficult to monitor. The issue is basically a political one. The Secretary of State for Education would have to go to the Cabinet and demand a direct *quid pro quo* for introducing what would be a sectionally unpopular scheme: and this would be finance from the Treasury for a defined scheme (such as implementation of Plowden) for raising the quality of primary and secondary education.

The savings

All exercises that have been undertaken on various loan schemes to assess the possible savings have been highly conjectural. The imponderables are endless, but the very fact that such a scheme would yield a net saving compared to the present prospect of ever-spiralling expenditure is sufficient to justify a scheme. The waiving of interest on the loan is a major concession, entailing a wait of up to ten years before appreciable savings are made and the necessity of a perpetual subsidy from then on depending upon the rate of expansion of the student population and the rate of price inflation. Subsidy would also be required to cover hardship cases. It is certain that without some graduates paying virtually a commercial rate for their loan, any thought of a self-liquidating scheme should be abandoned. But state subsidy is recognised in most loan scheme countries. And the fact that many students would not borrow or would only borrow a little and many would pay back early would help matters – to what extent it is impossible to say. It is even conceivable that a future government might feel obliged to introduce an interest charge, if only to cover the cost of further expansion of the scheme.

To hazard a guess, however: assuming the £100m. at present is treated as current outlay, not capital (in other words, no return was sought on it); assuming that early repayment, family support, and non-claimants from the scheme reduce the scale of the operation and balance the increase in the student population in the 'run-up' period to the steady state; and assuming that the subsidy basically covers inflation and further increases in student numbers, two-thirds of the present outlay should be being recouped in ten years' time, or £60m. to £70m. a year. A scheme of this sort, which is an extremely 'lenient' one, would never approach self-liquidation. But it would be recouping very substantial sums of money nonetheless, which would be pure gain as against the present system. They are sums which, on any showing, would be better put to use in other sectors of the education service to improve educational standards, reduce deprivation and promote equality of opportunity.

Any reallocation of priorities hurts somebody, and the one proposed here will leave many graduates worse off than they are at present. But reallocate we must if the education service (and higher education itself) is to continue to keep pace with growing numbers. A loans scheme is a perfectly workable and tolerable innovation and one that would release far greater potential resources than any other feasible reform. It should be implemented without delay.

BILL VAN STRAUBENZEE

the case *against* student loans

My first complaint against the case for student loans is the misleading language in which it is invariably cast. To describe the scheme as a system of student loans gives the impression that this is just a new method by which the government will pay for student maintenance. This is not so. The adoption of student loans would effectively compel students to pay for their own support. The fact that the government would arrange to make a bridging loan is an important but separate and secondary issue which should not be allowed to disguise the fact that the student would eventually be paying for his maintenance out of his own pocket. This makes it quite clear that the loans proposal is not a change of method, but a change of priorities, the shifting of the burden of maintenance from the government to the individual student.

No budgetary argument

I challenge the budgetary arguments on the widest possible front. Expenditure on higher education is not out of control; the loans proposal is not financially water-tight; it will not provide the budgetary relief so confidently predicted; and it would result in less efficient use of our existing higher education resources.

Higher education expenditure not out of control

Part of Simon Jenkins' argument is based on the premise that because higher education has grown at a faster rate than other sectors in recent years, it is by implication taking more than its fair share. I cannot rid my mind of his vision of the insatiable craw of higher education greedily consuming vast resources, thereby depriving primary and secondary education of the very crust on which to bite. *Statistics of Education* 1966 Volume 5 give the following figures for England and Wales. Between 1959-60 and 1965-6 expenditure on primary schools increased 65 per cent, secondary schools 67 per cent, further and adult education 129 per cent, teacher training 234 per cent, universities 198 per cent, and total expenditure (excluding meals and milk) 91 per cent. No one would deny that expenditure on higher education has multiplied at an unprecedented rate. But the reason for this is that it started from a small base. In 1959-60 further and adult education, teacher training and the universities absorbed only 23 per cent of education expenditure. By 1965-6 their percentage had grown to 32 per cent. There has been a growing realisation in the past decade that the school leaver is unskilled, untrained and ill-equipped to play a part in a modern technological society. It is still a cause for concern that in 1966 only 16.5 per cent of boys leaving school went on to some form of further or higher education. In order to raise this percentage, higher education expenditure will continue to rise rapidly each year.

There is no official projection as to the future cost of maintenance grants. However, there must be a very close correlation between the number of students expected to enter higher education and the cost of maintenance grants required to support them. In 1966-7 there were 339,000 students in higher education. Revised predictions suggest 420,000 to 470,000 in 1973-4 and somewhere between 600,000 and 750,000 by 1980-81. Taking the upper end of the range for both dates, the compound annual growth rate in student maintenance grants would still only be 5 per cent per annum to 1973-4 and 6 per cent to 1980-1. Expenditure on grants is going to grow at a substantial rate but these figures are certainly not out of control in relation to total expenditure on higher education. Maintenance grants are going to be expensive but not a runaway juggernaut.

Loans not financially watertight

If the arguments in favour of student loans are based on budgetary considerations, then it is essential to see precisely how successful the loan repayment system would be. Under the loan system we are discussing the government cannot hope to receive back all that it has lent.

Women graduates

First there are women graduates. They constitute a quarter of the student population in England and Wales and one-third in Scotland. Any attempt to saddle husbands with their wives' loan repayment is legally and politically quite unacceptable. A negative dowry of £1,200 is an idea completely alien to our legal system. Moreover, to introduce the problem of a student loan into marital arrangements would be an intolerable intrusion into personal relationships. Women graduates might be made subject to some form of contractual repayment rather than variable repayable advances, but it is certain that a woman could only be obliged to repay loans out of money she had received in her own right.

A proportion of women graduates do not go into employment on leaving higher education and a large number would leave employment to get married before their earnings reached the repayment threshold. Still more would leave employment before their loans were completely repaid. The government can expect to write off a material proportion of loans to women.

Emigrant graduates

Secondly, there are the British students who go abroad after graduation or before their earnings reach a high level. The authorities could treat these graduates in two ways. First they could forgo repayments while the student is abroad. This policy would be fatal since students would then have a positive incentive to emigrate in order to avoid their debt. Alternatively the government could convert the graduate's loan into a contractual debt compelling him to remit fixed instalments from his income abroad. This would be complex. In the event of default, the government's only practical remedy would be to refuse to renew the emigrant's passport.

There are of course many foreign-born students who qualify for LEA awards in this country but who intend returning home on completion of their studies. In these cases the government could whistle for its money.

Low paid graduates

We should not forget those who for one reason or another may never reach an earnings level sufficient for loan repayments to be completed. The clergy and some self-employed graduates will fall into this category. Moreover, there will also be cases where ill-health or physical disability prevents repayment.

Total amount recouped

Taking into account women students, emigrants, low paid graduates and those unable to repay, the DES might think itself lucky if, after the expenses of collection, it recouped as much as three-quarters of the amount originally lent.

The repayment schedule

If budgetary considerations are held to be important then early repayment of loans is essential. But in fact early repayment is not likely to be possible. On leaving university a graduate does not earn more than the average manual worker. A student entering industry can expect to earn £1,000 to £1,200 per year. Simon Jenkins' proposal that £50 should be repayable when annual income climbs over £1,000 and that the total should be repaid over twelve years seems quite acceptable.

On his own figures he claims that the saving ten years from now would only be running at £60m. to £70m. per year. This would be only about 2.5 per cent to 3 per cent of total annual expenditure on education at that time. Advocates of student loans are in effect arguing that we should completely upset the basis of our higher education system and discourage large sections of the community who are entering higher education for the first time, simply in order to save up to 3 per cent of national expenditure on education, not now, but in ten years time.

If loans were introduced for school leavers entering higher education in October 1968, the amount lent in 1968-9 would be about £35m. Borrowers would not leave university until the summer of 1971 at the earliest. Repayment of this £35m. would not get going until 1972 and would not be complete until the end of 1976. The total sum lent in the three years 1968-9 to 1970-1 would be only half repaid by the end of 1978 and would not be fully repaid until 1983. This is not instant budgetary relief. The argument that the funds released can be spent on educational purposes which now have a higher priority therefore hardly applies.

Moreover, these calculations ignore any interest charges. The government's cost of borrowing at present is about 7 per cent. Assume the student borrows about £400 in 1968-9 and the same additional amounts in 1969-70 and 1970-1. Assume further that repayment commences in 1972 and continues by rising instalments until completion in 1983. If a 7 per cent rate of interest were applied just to the amount outstanding at each stage of the study and repayment period, the total accumulated interest by 1983 would be £702.

The illusion of budgetary relief

The use of loans to replace maintenance grants would apparently save about £100m. or 5 per cent of national expenditure on education. If only three-quarters of sums lent are recouped, the saving would be 3.75 per cent. After deducting interest charges of £702 per £1,200, the saving would be down to 1.6 per cent. The government would not feel the first benefit of this saving until 1972. By 1983 a net saving of 1.6 per cent of the 1968-9 education bill will have been accomplished and the Treasury will then be congratulating itself on how well the system has worked.

Parental contributions

In the case for loans we were told that following their introduction, 'there can be no doubt that the amount of family income attracted into supporting students at university would increase substantially'. But is this so? If loans were introduced now many parents would immediately cease paying their parental contribution and tell their loving sons and daughters to borrow the lot from the government. The possible impact of this switch should not be underestimated: at the moment parental contributions are running at about £40m. a year.

Moreover, it is suggested that students should be allowed to borrow well over the new grant limit of £395. If the natural reaction is that parents stop their contribution and students borrow more than £395, then the government could actually find itself having to lend more money than it at present gives away. So much for instant budgetary relief.

Harmful effects on university efficiency

At university the student is bound to be conscious of the need to repay. The mere prospect of having to pay back instalments almost immediately after leaving university is a very sobering thought. It is undeniable that there would be greater pressure on the student to recoup the money he is spending while at university. Vacation jobs would become the necessity that they are in the United States and some parts of Europe. Some students would feel constrained to take term-time employment. The effects are difficult to quantify but would probably manifest themselves in two ways.

1. Longer academic courses

At the moment the British university course is about the shortest and most intensive in the world. The Robbins Report estimates the average time taken to complete a degree in Great Britain as 3.75 years. In Sweden the average is 4.75 years while in Germany,

Holland and France the figure is more like 5 or 6 years. If loans for maintenance force more students to take on jobs in term-time and in vacations, it can be expected that it will take them longer to complete their degree course. The result will be a decline in efficiency.

However, it must also be admitted that student loans would be a very effective stick to persuade students to complete their degree courses as soon as they possibly can.

2. Increased wastage and failure rates

If students feel the need to earn money while at university, their ability to study will be impaired and higher wastage and failure rates can be expected. This is especially so if academically weak students are unable to study in vacations. Appendix 5 of the Robbins Report suggests that wastage rates in other countries run as high as 30 per cent to 50 per cent or more. By comparison, at English and Welsh universities in 1966 the wastage rate was 18 per cent including 7.9 per cent failing an intermediate examination, 2.8 per cent failing the final examination and 5.2 per cent who terminated their course for other reasons.

Adverse effects after university

It is impossible to say categorically that graduate salaries would be inflated. Even if this did take place, it would not necessarily be a bad thing since it would simply mean that employers will be paying directly for the training of the skilled labour which they require. I suspect that it would not be long before the following advertisement appeared in *Graduate Careers*: 'Starting salary of £1100 plus repayment of any loan liability arising while in our employment'.

A more important point is that, in spite of the threshold system, students with a debt of £1,200 on their minds will certainly pay much more attention to the level of salary offered by their prospective employers. Employers offering uncompetitive salaries such as local government and the public services could find that this is the last straw. The teaching profession in particular may have to raise its bidding in order to attract graduates who have substantial loans to repay. Even a small rise in teachers' salaries costs a vast amount of money. If the introduction of students' loans necessitated an increase in teachers' salaries, most of the financial savings brought through loans would be wiped out at one stroke.

Taxation

As mentioned in the introduction, repayment of loans through the tax system will add to the marginal tax rate of graduates in management and the professions. This is contrary to the widely accepted need to reduce the disincentive effect of high marginal tax rates.

A high proportion of graduates are self-employed, for example as lawyers, doctors, journalists, authors and artists. PAYE is not applicable to the self-employed. Repayment in all these cases would require yet another schedule in the annual income tax return. The Inland Revenue would have to maintain a register of taxpayers' academic qualifications in order to prevent evasion.

Wrong in principle

So far the arguments have dealt with why loans may not work in practice. Now something must be said on why student loans are wrong in principle.

Anderson and Robbins

The most authoritative investigation into methods of student support was that of the Anderson Committee which reported in May 1960. That report[1] devoted only one-third of a page to loans:

> 'We were, however, struck by the official use of the system of loans to students in, among other countries, Norway and the United States and we felt it right to consider the merits of some such system; but though we recognise that a loan may occasionally be a reasonable way of meeting a particular difficulty, we have had no hesitation in rejecting loans as an integral part of the national awards system. The principle of using loans as a standard means of financing students has now been abandoned by public authorities in Great Britain and our evidence disclosed no wish to see it revived. The obligation to repay, no matter how easy the terms, must represent an untimely burden at the outset of a career. We far prefer the system of outright grants, with the safeguards against misuse, contained in our recommendations.'

The Robbins Report discusses loans on pages 210 to 212 and reaches the following conclusion:

> 'On balance we do not recommend immediate recourse to a system of financing students by loans. At a time when many parents are only just beginning to acquire the habit of contem-

[1] 'Grants for Students', Cmnd No. 1051. April 1960.

> plating higher education for such of their children, especially girls, as are capable of benefiting by it, we think it probable that it would have undesirable disincentive effects. But if, as time goes on, the habit is more firmly established, the arguments of justice in distribution and of the advantage of increasing individual responsibility may come to weigh more heavily and lead to some experiment in this direction.'

The deterrent effect of loans

The abandonment of grants and their replacement by loans which the student will eventually repay must be a disincentive to school leavers from low income families. And we should not underestimate the importance of the present system of grants to less wealthy students. The NUS estimates that about half the student population is receiving maximum or near maximum grants and about one-third of students in full-time higher education come from manual workers' families. Many of them are only able to take part in higher education because they are not called upon to pay for their maintenance. The simple fact is that grants are an attractive subsidy whereas loans are a deterrent, even though they may be repayable out of income in later life. At the first European Conference of UNESCO in Vienna in November 1967, Mrs Shirley Williams, Minister of State, Department of Education and Science said:

> 'Our relative success in widening the social range of students obviously follows to some extent from the widening opportunities in secondary education, which is available on a similar basis in all parts of the country, and which is, of course, free even beyond the compulsory leaving age. But the other important factor is the generous system of student awards in Britain. We finance students in all three types of higher education by outright grants and not by loans.'

Instead of giving equality of opportunity to students from rich and poor families alike, loans are certain to give the middle class student an advantage. We know that Simon Jenkins intends loan repayments to be as painless as possible so that they need not be a genuine worry to the less-well-off school leaver. But it is nevertheless true that under a loan system a higher degree of enterprise will be required from both the student and his parents before embarking on a higher education course. That enterprise will not always be forthcoming. Even though the student himself will be prepared to undertake the burden of a student loan, parents may be averse to the whole idea. In discussing loans the danger is that we are drawn into abstruse arguments about cost/benefit analysis, lifetime earnings etc. when what really matters is equality of opportunity. Student loans would result in a decline in the proportion of graduates from working class families.

It is argued that money 'saved' by the introduction of student loans should be used on other aspects of education, and in particular to improve the position of underprivileged children while still at school. There would certainly be greater equality of opportunity if we spent more money on Plowden's educational priority areas, on secondary school education in poor districts and on maintenance grants for working class sixth formers.

But it is a sick joke to propose that the money for these improvements should be found by severing the ladder of opportunity at the age of eighteen. In blunt terms, it is no good encouraging children from low-income families to stay on at school until they are sixteen or eighteen, if you are going to slam the door in their face at the precise moment when they are in greatest need of tangible financial assistance. I can think of no policy which would be more successful in shattering the aspirations of young people.

The benefit argument

One of the strongest cases for loans is that graduates benefit directly from the expensive education which they receive and should therefore be called upon to pay for it instead of the burden falling on the community as a whole. There is an undeniable element of truth in this but the argument is not as simple as it sounds.

First there is the obvious point that if graduates do benefit financially from their education, then our progressive taxation system ensures that they pay back much or all of the amount spent on their higher education.

Second, the education received benefits society as a whole and not only the graduates themselves.

Third, we must take account of the fact that in order to receive later financial rewards graduates sacrifice at least six years of full-time economic earnings, i.e., from the age of fifteen to twenty-one.

Graduates' higher salaries may be due to their greater innate ability, effort or initiative rather than to the education received. Many graduates would be earning above average incomes even without higher education and it is impossible to establish how much of a graduate's income is attributable to his qualifications alone.

Once these four factors are taken into consideration the 'benefit argument' loses much of its strength.

Distortion effect on courses and subjects

The introduction of loans is certain to have distorting effects on students' choice of subjects and courses. The four-year first degree course – such as that at Keele University – would disappear virtually overnight since there is no point in a student paying £1600 for a course which would cost him £1200 elsewhere. Medicine and dentistry would be similarly vulnerable owing to the length of these courses. Much post-graduate and research work would collapse since students could not countenance the accumulation of large amounts of debt over four or five years. The only way a student could carry on post-graduate or research work would be by finding an academic institution, government department or industrial company which would employ him to do it. It would be rare to find post-graduates pursuing academic work without strings attached.

The recruitment and training of teachers must suffer badly if students in colleges of education are forced to borrow money to pay for their maintenance. It has to be admitted that free tuition and free maintenance in colleges of education are a major means of attracting suitable young people into the profession. To charge trainee teachers for their maintenance would have a catastrophic effect on recruitment. The effect would be so serious that it is almost inevitable that the government would have to reintroduce grants for teacher trainees.

Once an exception is made for teachers, it is likely that grants would be reintroduced to give special support to those subjects and courses which had been hardest hit by the introduction of loans. Such measures would not be intolerable but they would at least be an unhappy complication. The result would be serious discrimination between courses and a marked reduction in the money which the government would expect to 'save.'

Conclusion

The net saving following introduction of student loans would be very small in relation to the £2,000m. now spent on education each year. Moreover, it would be ten years before savings would really become available for other purposes. In the meantime grants are crucial to our policy of encouraging a wider section of the community to enter higher education. Student grants are socially and educationally necessary and they are an expenditure which we can and will afford.

There may come a day when our standard of living is so high, and higher education so widely accepted amongst all classes of the community, that student grants will no longer be required. That day has not yet arrived.

THE AUTHORS

Simon Jenkins read PPE at St John's College, Oxford, and did post-graduate work at the University of Sussex before becoming research assistant at the University of London Institute of Education. He is now News Editor of *The Times Educational Supplement* and a governor of the Archbishop Tenison's School, London. He was author of the Bow Group memorandum *Conservatives and comprehensives* (CPC, 1967).

William van Straubenzee, MBE, MP, who has been the Member for Wokingham since 1959, was Parliamentary Private Secretary to the Minister of Education from 1960 to 1962. He is Chairman of the Governors of Archbishop Tenison's School, London; an Honorary Vice-President of the National Union of Students; and Honorary Secretary of the Federation of Conservative Students.